DEAR FUTURE

Also by Jennifer Richter:

Threshold
No Acute Distress

Dear Future

Jennifer Richter

THE WORD WORKS
WASHINGTON, D. C.

Dear Future © 2024 Jennifer Richter

Reproduction
of this book in any form
or by any means, electronic
or mechanical, except when quoted
in part for the purpose of review,
must be with permission in
writing from the publisher.
Address inquiries to
THE WORD WORKS

P.O. Box 42164
Washington, D.C. 20015
editor@wordworksbooks.org
Author photograph: Luke Scribner
Cover photograph: Vicki Jauron
Cover design: Susan Pearce

ISBN: 978-1-944585-69-3
LCCN: 2024930015

Acknowledgments

My deep gratitude to the editors of the publications in which these poems, sometimes in earlier versions, first appeared:

The Account: "Trending: Seismologist Explains How to Make an Earthquake Early Warning System with Cats" and "Message in a Bottle: Dear Future"
CALYX Journal: "Back in the Saddle" and "Quarantine Telehealth Well-Woman Profile"
Entropy: "Years ago we told her It's okay to have some things that you don't share"
The Los Angeles Review: "Elegy with Aftershocks, Late and Soon"
The Massachusetts Review: "The Underworld Also Swallows Sons"
The Missouri Review: "Love Poem Grounded in the Seismic Communication of Elephants"
Moss: "Over Oregon the Flight Attendant Asks If I'm Interested in Water"
Nimrod: "I Feel You" and "Shout-Out to the Little Girl Bear-Walking Through TSA Security"
South Dakota Review: "Imagine that: I need this + I'm good at getting this = I got this"
Sweet Lit: "Still Life with Earthquake Weather and Blueberries"
Unlost Journal: "To Tell a Different Story You Try a Different Mouth (Seismologist Cento)"
ZYZZYVA: "Everywhere we go people want to know" and "On Wanting to Be One More Time a Survivable Void Space for My Son"

Thanks

Thanks to so many, my life feels full of love and luck and light. My deep gratitude to Felicia Zamora for hearing these poems clearly, for writing about them with such insight and affection, and for giving them a home outside of me.

Thank you to Nancy White, Kasey Jueds, and Jennifer Barber—my editorial dream team—and to Karren Alenier, Susan Pearce, Marilyn McCabe, and everyone in the Word Works family for their expertise and enthusiasm. To my publicist Mary Bisbee-Beek for her belief in this book, her persistence, and constant good cheer.

Thank you to Bruce Weigl and Diane Seuss for their extraordinary generosity and their poems that teach me to speak from the dark, say something that gleams.

I'm profoundly grateful for my parents' unwavering love and support; for my big, beautiful Texas family; for my beloved longtime poetry family David Keplinger, Colleen Morton Busch, B.T. Shaw, and Molly Spencer, and for my amazing chosen family, Amy Burrows, Kris Nugent, Jotham Burrello, Rachel Kirby, and Shannon Keon, each of whom has carried inside them, for decades, the most generous version of me.

Thank you to my Oregon State students and colleagues, especially Karen Holmberg, David Biespiel, Anna Fidler, Felicia Phillips, Ray Malewitz, and Dana Reason, who buoy and inspire me. Many thanks, too, to the OSU Center for the Humanities for awarding me a fellowship at just the right time, and to Loma Karklins and Peter Collopy at the Caltech Archives.

To Luke and Chloe and your huge, resilient hearts. What a tremendous privilege it is to be your mom; what an incredible gift, to be invited into your daily lives. This book exists because of your ongoing trust. Thank you. I love you. There will always be room for you in me.

And to Keith—by my side for half my life now—who tethers me to my very best self, whose adventurous spirit rallies me, whose boundless love settles and sustains me, and whose hand in mine makes me brave. There's so much to come. You, dear one, are why my horizon shines.

Contents

Introduction by Felicia Zamora / 1

~

Trending: Seismologist Explains How to Make an Earthquake Early
    Warning System with Cats / 7
Over Oregon the Flight Attendant Asks If I'm Interested in Water / 9
On Wanting to Be One More Time a Survivable Void Space for My Son / 10
The Underworld Also Swallows Sons / 12
To Tell a Different Story You Try a Different Mouth (Seismologist Cento) / 13
Still Life with Earthquake Weather and Blueberries / 16
Everywhere we go people want to know / 17

~

Love Poem Grounded in the Seismic Communication of Elephants / 21
#momlife #mood #meow / 22
Elegy with Aftershocks, Late and Soon / 23
Imagine that: I need this + I'm good at getting this = I got this / 24
Every Mother Since Demeter Scours the Earth for Cracks / 25
Years ago we told her It's okay to have some things that you don't share / 26
Under the Surface / 27

~

Erasing "The Really Big One" (My Therapist Suggests I Practice
    Reframing) / 31

~

Back in the Saddle / 41
Quarantine Telehealth Well-Woman Profile / 42
How's Your Day So Far / 43
reading a book of poetry there are spaces between the words
    i think about hitting the world with a rubber hammer / 45
Blackberry, Blackberry, Blackberry / 46
I Feel You / 47
Gone Viral / 48
America Completes Its 100-Word Interest Inventory with Permitted
    Items Found on TSA's "What Can I Bring?" Website / 49

Shout-Out to the Little Girl Bear-Walking Through TSA Security   /   53
It's Time for Them to Go Again   /   54
Mailing Care Packages on the Day the Barcelona Opera House
       Reopens with a Concert Exclusively for 2,292 Plants   /   55
Do beavers even know what they're doing or do they just see water
       flowing down a river and think "absolutely not"   /   56
Here Comes the Sun   /   58
Still Life with Clear Skies and Blueberries   /   59
Love Wave   /   60
Message in a Bottle: Dear Future   /   61

Notes   /   63
About the Author   /   About the Artist   /   65
About The Word Works   /   67
About the Tenth Gate Prize   /   Past Winners   /   68

Introduction

"Some believe the earth is a big body / that shakes sometimes." In *Dear Future*, we see the everyday quaked open to expose the seams of life's uncertainty. Each poem becomes its own magnitude of scale—its own pulsating seismologic wave of language—that breaks loose for us to experience. These poems slide on a tightrope of moments compounded by imagery, ideation, and a slickness of language to portal us through space and time. With breath weaving ultimate control over many of these deliciously unpunctuated poems, we feel a building toward the interrogation of language, motherhood, and the covenants of "natural disaster or lasting love."

Our acts of daily practice become how we connect in this world; how we feel less toppled over from all that tries to shake us raw. Like seismology, the poem becomes the voice's science, "I make this prayer in experiment / let me be less uncertain in my mind / unafraid / of words." From texting cat memes to a son and daughter, to communing with Charles Richter's journals, to cutting "dreams out of poems," to holding one's breath from being haunted by a son's depression and the fear of losing him, to Seismologist Centos, to an elephant's toenail conducting the earth's trembles, to the aftershocks of grief, to subduction zones, to quarantine telehealth sessions, we are shook in these poetic worlds. Shook, eyes agape.

Here the palimpsest of future predictions lives in the embrace of uncertainty and the rupture of language where, "seismologists agree meanwhile we chase hints / of what and when like red laser dots we won't / ever pin down." We slide from one cognitive thread to another in the fibers of voices thinking their way to persistent, necessary creation, where "We / fit together as tectonic plates do— / one of those rare natural puzzles."

—Felicia Zamora
Author of *I Always Carry My Bones*

For Luke and Chloe

Given my personal characteristics it is language that I must use to move my world.

—Charles F. Richter,
 creator of the earthquake magnitude scale

Trending: Seismologist Explains How to Make an Earthquake Early Warning System with Cats

Lately I have more cats in my Cloud than kids
in real life two kids no cats but now no kids at
home so cats are how we stay in touch if their
phones ring they huff mom why're you calling
but when I text my son a tabby in a taco bowtie
he texts right back maybe a chonky ginger and
I know he's okay that's a thumbs up for today
since the kids left I've been using cats to predict
disaster as the seismologist says it's tricky you'd
think cats parkouring through kitchens crashing
trashing everything would mean it's all falling
apart you'd think a cat reeling with cheese stuck
to its face might be a cry for help but when he
sends those I know my son's actually laughing
that day my daughter had a fever and a French
final I texted you're the best with a mustached
Munchkin she sent back a show-posed golden
Persian someone had captioned yo for real this
cat looks like the grandfather of a croissant how
is it only 16th best ha I thought okay she's okay
when they don't respond I'm suddenly back
in a too-quiet house with toddlers I worry if
one sends the same meme two days in a row
what's so distracting I worry getting bursts of
Norwegian Forest cats in the snow from my son
it's tricky you'd think all those dreamy scenes
might mean he'd found a little peace this week
but the last winter he lived at home it vanished
the neighbor's cat with ears like that slept only
on our deck only ever let my son get close then
one day left no warning just didn't come back
that winter my friend left too you never know
seismologists agree meanwhile we chase hints

of what and when like red laser dots we won't
ever pin down a guy online actually analyzed
a thousand cookie fortunes found very few use
predictive language mostly they offer random
observations about you like my daughter when
I visit her wow mom at my outfit means either
the heart-eyed cat emoji or the crying one now
my son texts kittens spilled from a takeout box
rice like snow on their noses my friend's hands
on my body used to shake with jolts that rose
he said from deep beneath his feet okay you'll
be okay he said anyone can heal anyone then
pointed to a shadowed corner sighing oh look
at all their wings so I squinted like I do at my
phone now at one of the sticky snarling kittens
chewing a fortune you are surrounded by angels
it says wow mom they'd say if my kids saw me
always staring at my dark screen like that corner
look I'd say I'm okay every day you light it up

Over Oregon the Flight Attendant Asks If I'm Interested in Water

> *I was wondering how you feel about your name being associated with a disaster.* —fan mail to seismologist Charles Francis Richter

Over Oregon the flight attendant asks if I'm interested in water
and I nod at his tray of clear cups lined up like the carnival game

that won me a fish I named after myself oh like the Richter scale
people say in Oregon where tsunami trips kids up on spelling tests

some letters are absurd they ask the seismologist *which of these states
should I move to* but one begins *you are the only other Francis I know*

*my teacher told me about you I hate my name because kids joke about it
I don't even have a middle name I can use what do your friends call you*

do earthquakes scare you like they do me yes thanks I'm very interested
in the unlikely event of water landing on our home thirty thousand

feet below when I chose to keep this name disaster hadn't occurred
to me but here all children drop cover hold on in school ours raised

their hands to my husband's name on the first day the teacher never
knew who I belonged to their hair matches exactly that class goldfish

with alarmed eyes if something happens how will strangers help me
find them my name will be useless my name will be news for years

that third-grade fish has been living dying getting replaced overnight
though to the children it's always Charlie the seismologist's name

ended with him but his carbon-copied reply calls the boy son and
uses the word *wonder* when ours was lost in the children's museum

he'd looped back to the tsunami tank to methodically stack blocks
under a giant timer counting down to the wave that came so close

he couldn't hear me calling

On Wanting to Be One More Time a Survivable Void Space for My Son

I used to cut dreams out of poems
used to cut out my 150 mg b.i.d.
once a year and think maybe now
my brain's blackout shade will rise
by itself maybe my son won't need
to know this about me but I was
dreaming obviously everyone said
yes they'd seen him yes he's really
depressed but I couldn't find my son
in the crowd the back of every head
was his then one man raised his arm
to point me down dream street but
stopped said wait you don't look
enough like him to be his mom
make a face you have in common
how would he answer how are you
when my son's doctor calls he calls
me mom says mom can you tell me
what medication you take because
there's a good chance your son will
respond to that nineteen years ago
he wasn't responding I'd said yes
to drugs hours earlier which maybe
was why his heart needed monitoring
when the doctor aimed a tiny wire at
my son's slick still-in-me head he said
keep breathing I remember back then
my son used to cry for one of three
reasons my body knew each answer
now he's crying but not hungry he's
tired but not sleeping never sleeping
scared but can't say why he's crying
happiest with the neighbor's old cat
that sits and stares like my son does

at our bunny hutch that's been empty
for ten months for so long I've been
holding my breath today for fifty-five
seconds I watched the wildfire blaze-
and-bunny video and started reaching
for the screen I'm that man panicking
that man thinking no one's watching
thinking how is this not a dream how
can I get him to sleep my son used to
sleep on me like a bunny on my belly
please if anyone out there is watching
deliver my son once more into light
this time I can catch him that first time
I couldn't wait to hear him cry

The Underworld Also Swallows Sons

The old couch cushion tipped you toward him;
hunched and skeletal, he didn't make a dent.
See how that could feel to him like pressure?
(His therapist, gently.) *But* (her quick glance,
his nod, negotiations with the god)
he'll tell you if he can't keep himself safe.
Walking out he lagged: a toddler again,
pocketing rocks. (To sink or settle him?
You can't ask.) In that one he's kept for years
you see its perfect hole is now a mouth:
pained, empty as a wound that's shot clean through.
He'll leave his room to eat with you, she said.
His door's a rift: half open, one flight down.
You watch that silence for his shadow's drift.

To Tell a Different Story You Try a Different Mouth (Seismologist Cento)

Charles F. Richter journal entry, 6/20/26:
> It was a surfeit of scientific occupation which led some years ago to a breakdown of my nerves…

1

Only one step

to go

so calmly there I stood upon the ledge

that for the moment I was half

alive

it was the realization of the artistic, or as I called it then, the spiritual aspect of the world, which first raised me out of that depression…

2

I make this prayer in experiment

let me be less uncertain in my mind

unafraid

of words

listen

just out beyond the circle of my light

they are all here

and it was the final accomplishment of self-expression in poetry which at last permitted me to return to my work.

3

At last

as if I were to turn the rusty locks

the sound of poetry

at the door

my friend

at last

you came

Still Life with Earthquake Weather and Blueberries

Since its last fruit we've been consumed. Still, without
pruning, sawdust mulch, or glance, our bush came back.
Just-picked berries hold the heat of our son's cheeks,
sobbing. Still. All along he's said he wants to live.

Everywhere we go people want to know

how he's doing and because we don't have
a new answer or two-second true answer
we can bear to admit we mostly don't go
anywhere mostly we've been watching
the cedar show all week across the street
three huge trees dangling orange men
total chainsaw circus we used to picnic
by any construction site we could find
crackers juice boxes his stuffed animals
propped up facing the scrape roar dump
and lurch of dust today a kindergarten
class comes to watch I hear them first
chanting over the machinery's racket
*WE ARE THE GECKOS   WE ARE THE GECKOS
MIGHTY MIGHTY GECKOS   MIGHTY MIGHTY
GECKOS* he used to love that picture book
gecko-hero licking dust off its own eyeball
I love their tiny voices shouting mighty
shouting you can talk yourself into being
brave just use your words your outside
voice I've started hearing everything
as a message in the lopped-off trunks
the neighbors' tree house is a little ark
snagged and dry above the waterline
in bed each night we clutch each other
steady ourselves on the rocking deck
below us our sleepless son thrashes
like an animal we didn't dream we'd be
at sea this long didn't dream he might
always struggle to stay above the dark
dark waves my heart sinking my heart
racing I'll always be listening like prey
for sounds of what's coming a warning
a voice Noah was given years to prepare

and exact plans this number of cubits
equals your family will all be fine but
all this morning's headlines offer me is
"A Rule of Thumb: If You See a Tsunami
It's Too Late to Outrun It" the new siren
drills in our town a comfort let's practice
not panicking let's keep looking for signs
the new ones at low points on the coast
are blue cartoons an open-mouthed huge
wave and stick figure scrambling away
we used to chant good job at everything
he did without our help first he learned
to cry himself to sleep we used to follow
what the books said turns out that works
he's still really good at it and we're still
standing outside his door listening silently
crying some books call his pain a journey
he has to take alone but the chirping geckos
hand in hand on the sidewalk are counting
off by twos Noah did what the voice said
good job it said to save them pair them up

Love Poem Grounded in the Seismic Communication of Elephants

So who do we know that's happily married
you ask in bed tonight after two more dear
friends split. We're quiet awhile, lie baffled
by the largest silence of our lives: no more
desk chairs rumbling upstairs; no phones
thunked to the hardwood at 2am, slipped
from our sleeping children's hands. Empty
nest, week one, I needed noise; at the fair
I bought clay elephants. Artist: age eight.
Sold only as a pair. Just like ours, I thought:
the smaller one who doesn't miss a thing,
its ears like two full sails; the other's head
tipped and listening, its trunk curled into
a question. Our son around that age said
elephants can sense what's coming. Asked
if we knew. His best friend's dad had just
moved out and left their house a wreck.
What's coming is sometimes a tsunami,
sometimes the beloved mate's vibration.
Nights now when we touch and shudder,
we let our echoes stampede every room.
This gray clay couple grown to look alike:
of course they're not the kids. Same flat
feet as ours, same wrinkly skin, all ears
except our future comes as a constant
surprise. Who knew? The elephants'
bones conduct the music when they
listen—the earth's movement trembles
in their toenails, then pulses up their
skeleton's vast map to the inner ear
which recognizes the low frequency
of natural disaster or lasting love.

#momlife #mood #meow

I worry about my kids finding their people
I've spent hours scrolling through profiles
of adoptable cats that answer in first person
the shelter's second-date hot-seat questions
how would you describe yourself are you
comfortable being alone how do you feel
about kids I hear my own so clearly hi I'm
charmingly chatty the life of the paw-ty but
also a couch cuddler a super loyal lovebug
hi I'm purrfectly happy on laps and laptops
mr. handsome a real softie once I've adjusted
I'll be your trusty sidekick on the road of life
some cats say I'm excited to put the past in
my rearview mirror not sure how my kids
would answer what was your previous home
like and because of that what do you need
now if I'm their very first home what does
that mean they'll need from their forever
people so many out there waiting so many
bonded pairs when you realize it's time
to put your cats in the care of others to re-
home them the shelter calls it surrendering

Elegy with Aftershocks, Late and Soon

for Jon Tribble (1962-2019) and Allison Joseph

I just had my seismic sense implants removed [from my feet]. I've been sensing earthquakes for the last 7 years ... and I'm now feeling phantom earthquakes.
　—Moon Ribas, Facebook, 6/19/19

Some believe the earth is a big body
that shakes sometimes like ours with
fever or seizure or the rare tremor of
its heart we think we can predict we
think we can prepare but in the end
it's the body that decides three days
after you'd gone a West Coast quake
rose from miles below you always
felt that deeply that strongly maybe
for those few like you at some point
the world is too much with them
a woman with wide wise eyes like
your wife's tells the news *Before the
shaking what woke me sounded like a
door slamming like someone just left*
then she sighs *Something is shaking
all the time now but maybe it's just me*

Imagine that: I need this + I'm good at getting this = I got this

So many people I love don't know what to do
me neither so I watch live coverage of a bear
catching salmon in Alaska 2.1 K watching too
also commenting so I know his name is Otis
and this is his spot his office someone calls it
Otis scans the surface churn and waits surely
he's starving that's four in ten minutes but he
doesn't panic GO BEAR GO someone says as
Otis pounces in slo-mo LIKE A BOSS another
says snorkel snorkel snorkel when Otis sinks
his snout then nom nom nom to his sparkly
squirming mouthful a new viewer says once
in a play my son was called Juicy Salmon #2
and the chat erupts with laugh-crying emojis
when my son calls his cried-out voice sounds
underwater if only he could feel for a while
whatever he wants swimming towards him
so much of it that he'd need a break like our
Otis splayed in the shallows he just reached
out and snagged one hi everybody someone
says it's so nice knowing people are around
suddenly the chat stops scrolling not sure
which yellow face to click we made a deal
my son can answer me with a single emoji
my question is always are you still around
he didn't mean to die my friend's husband
left their TV on like this rushing whitewater
like late night static also gone like the sound
that quit helping me sleep it's a struggle just
to keep going I know so many like my son
feel caught in the jaws of something larger

Every Mother Since Demeter Scours the Earth for Cracks

> after Walter De Maria's 1977 art installation *The New York Earth Room*

Even onscreen it settles me
this solid wall-to-wall soil
undisturbed and guarded
one hundred and forty tons
of black horizon line filling
the loft's bare white rooms
to the sills to the knee-high
plexiglass in one doorway
where visitors stand their
kids stoop to palm that flat
view like a cross-sectioned
zoo habitat long abandoned
four decades later the work's
still here outliving its artist
same simple goal of mothers
scanning each stretch of earth
so quiet complains one critic
another too predictable what
mother doesn't covet peace
and routine what kid doesn't
plead just a little longer at the
zoo I'd get so tired of standing
at the famous rodent's exhibit
the one with naked in its name
that made my rapt daughter
giggle its info plaque bragging
I'm a legendary tunneller look
my underground chambers are
just like rooms in your home
and fun fact I live here with a
queen who wasn't born a queen

Years ago we told her It's okay to have some things that you don't share

Slouching groggy down the stairs she startles when she sees me
Oh wait Mama you were an actual ghost next to the bed last night
like those what're they called holograms all floaty but your same
robe same scrunchie but your hair was actual feathers then you
just started dissolving oh wait sorry is this weird for you to hear
and I shake my head amazed by what she trusts me with amazed
because I hadn't mentioned the robin that burst from our branches
when the tree crew got too close she vanished with one blue egg
in her beak I'd never seen that I don't expect to know everything
so I looked online but the chats said no they don't do that it's not
in their nature that couldn't have happened that never happened
today she leaves again for the bedroom she's started calling home
I know someday a chatroom-chainsaw voice may try to silence her
I think she knows that whatever she tells me I'll say I believe you
sweetie I'll always open my mouth for you

Under the Surface

> *A Long-Lost Cupid Is Revealed Under the Surface of One of Vermeer's Greatest Paintings*
> —artnet.com, 5/8/19

I want to be remembered most for making
our daughter and son they're masterpieces
we've been admiring in our home for years
the diffused glow of their curls their cheeks
radiant as Vermeer's girl reading a window-
lit letter like ours on her illuminated screen
same indecipherable expression both girls
scanning for words they want from anyone
not their mom hovering right there Cupid's
got her back the winged god staring at me
bow in hand mask underfoot a giant defiant
toddler standing on his toys refusing to give
up on me years ago when I loved a boy for
sharing his sailboat his cars his family's
estate where his groomed poodle heeled
as he led me down hushed and dustless
hallways pausing at every painting she
tilted her head to his docent tone it's true
there was so much I wasn't seeing Cupid
it's been ages I'm so glad you're back
my daughter's weeping again she's me
before you aimed me away from a Still
Life as Vermeer's Foregrounded Fruit
upset like that forever my god you know
how tough this is to watch I recognize
you're my cue to back out of the picture
I know you know how wrong that feels

Erasing "The Really Big One" (My Therapist Suggests I Practice Reframing)

> *(Laughs.) Well, I wouldn't move. I mean, I still live here.*
> —Chris Goldfinger, Oregon State University paleoseismologist featured in the *New Yorker* article "The Really Big One"

> *Usually one gets what one expects, but very rarely in the way one expected it.*
> —seismologist Charles F. Richter

0-1.9: Micro

*An earlier version of this article misstated how long we have and what we

> (looking at
> the
> clock
> hand
> all day long,
> that
> wave)

expected.

> (The
> new
> face
>
> of
> the
> future's
> watch
>
> is
> deep
> relief.)

2.0-3.9: Minor

What breaks quickly generally mends:
hearts

and everything else
wave-
like

that
a grown man is knocked over by.

4.0-4.9: Light

Being
loved
is
the closest to being
the original
flooding—
people
behaving like
seemingly solid
structures
until
together
they
slide off
their foundations.

5.0-5.9: Moderate

When/
if it happens:

a long, suspended, what-was-that moment
(no early warning,
a sudden jolt
radiating outward)
will be
the first sign
of

love,

too.

6.0-6.9: Strong

We
fit together as tectonic plates do—
one of those rare natural puzzles.
You reach;
I
quiver,
feeling this sort of
midnight-
sofa-
moving
magnitude,
all
minor
and
major
subduction zones
(all the right anatomical parts,
in other words)
heating up
below,
one
plate
eventually
sliding deep beneath....

Geologists explain,
our
field
has
the sexiest
regions
to uncover.

7.0-7.9: Major

To
a place in a long period of quiet,
the Pacific Northwest:
remarkably benign
and
temperate
for millennia—

this is
a
toast.

To
the northwest edge of the continent, from California to Canada!
Like us
it is young
as continent stuff goes,
not
slipping steadily.

8.0-9.9: Great

"Doing
what
is
right"
is
where
our
name comes from.

Richter

is
more than
magnitude.

10.0+: Epic (never been recorded)

In the end
what was coming

was pretty cool, a real-time revolution
proving
the planet was
(applause)
stronger than
seismologists had believed:

in amazement,
lurching,
the body
itself was
making a strange rattling sound

on
the day
when
6.9
billion
people
(everyone)

after all
began to laugh

everyone

shaking

Back in the Saddle

On days I think he needs a gentle push
I go way back to his first two-wheeled try:
me steadying his seat, about to run
beside him but with one strong pedal-lunge
he's off, alone—a warm wind in his place.
The space they left in me when they were born
is where I carry our grown children's pain.
They let me hold them that way, still. They call.
Two years ago he crashed, grips waffling
his palms as he held on exhausted, lost.
A darkness fell on him. His voice got flat,
so thin, a broken spoke. The rough path back:
I've been there, know the practicing it takes
each morning trying to get up. Lately
my son makes healing look easy. Painless.
Just like riding a bike. The only truth
to that: some things, our bodies won't forget.
Now he wheelies everywhere, on winding
riverwalks, in downtown rush-hour traffic,
slaloming orange cones as strangers fumble
for their phones and wave. To be that picture
of balance—sure as years ago—I know
he pulls himself up many times each day.
No matter where I am I'm on the curb,
cheering. Incredible, how much he's grown.
Each time he breezes by, I feel his heat.
Like when he stoops, still lets me kiss his cheek.

Quarantine Telehealth Well-Woman Profile

No I'm not planning any more
pregnancies since in dog years
I'm 8 in cats I'm what they call
mature and also mostly indoor
so no I'm not concerned about
seasonal allergies or my alcohol
consumption yes I use caffeine
though in French somehow I'm
still très fatiguée no I haven't left
the country recently in airplanes
I'm most like a malfunctioning
pressure release valve yes I do
take deep breaths vitamins and
my frustrations out on others
on the scale of Band-Aid to 911
I'm a three-star fridge review
kinda frosty but fine could be
quieter now if we're talking
perishables I'd say I'm shrink-
wrapped meat I'm getting old
I'm on the edge of going bad
wait what even is today's date

How's Your Day So Far

Honestly exactly like that circus act
last night the aging clown drumroll
please sticking cutlery into various
holes his face has been kind enough
to provide first he licks his lips over
a giant plastic swordfish plattered
on his tiny bistro table why the long
fishface because it's detachable look
click snap he helicopters the blade
over his head then chop chop chop
look how it juliennes actual carrots
gasp then he opens his stance opens
wide for that shine that knifes down
inside him down up gulp clap clap
clap he bows bows then mimes oh
my manners I haven't cleaned my
plate examining the carrot shards
he points one finger in the air wait
pockets his foam nose sticks a fork
in his actual one not done yet oh no
slides the fork slowly straight back
into his sinuses flaunts his profile
examines the tines cross-eyed then
shuffles into the stands gone silent
finds a guy bats his eyes okay dear
right this way table for two hustles
him to the spotlight pulls his chair
out pours some bubbly licks his lips
then tilts his head and stabs a carrot
leans over the candelabra and waits
there drumroll please he waits like
that for his date who's increasingly
actually booed wow tough crowd
till he leans in and actually eats off

forkface gasp gulp clap clap thanks
for asking honestly today I'm both
that man chewing all the way back
to his seat and that sweaty clown
all three of us heading home hurt
in hidden places ladies and gents
today a whole room turned on me
flipped their painted-on grins boo
ouch wow tough crowd turns out
I'm great at swallowing everything
tada I'm bottomless as a top hat or
a deep sequined sleeve see inside
me are yards of knotted scarves a
skittery rabbit a new trick bouquet
this bad taste in my mouth from it
wilting on cue today its fake wiry
stems bent in half sucker-punched
each time I tried to give it away

reading a book of poetry there are spaces between the words i think about hitting the world with a rubber hammer

—title of 3-star Amazon book review

did you know hammering non-nail
things typically makes more space
isn't this year already broken enough
who out there isn't already shattered
good hammerers are precise maybe
you mean a rubber mallet not sure
rubber hammers are actually a thing
raise your hand if you're not sure you
exist rubber mallets sure are great at
undenting stuff under our apple tree
losing its fruit our dead car's hood is
getting wrecked raise your hand if
you're having trouble moving maybe
I need a new hobby maybe hard cider
in terms of day drinking the words
hammered shattered and wrecked
are the same basically I need apples
yeast and time imagine only needing
apples yeast and time who imagined
yeast would be the dealbreaker who
else feels like this pandemic is some
long weird season it's too hot to bake
but our driveway smells just like pie
one fall we forgot to prune the apple
tree and here's the thing come spring
between its branches it didn't have
any space and apparently that's just
how   pests   like it

Blackberry, Blackberry, Blackberry

*Longing, we say, because desire is full
of endless distances.*
                —Robert Hass

Our country fiery with virus, temp
hitting a hundred and two here but
my parked car displays one eleven,
all the new thinking: still about loss
when he crosses the lot—a coveralled
man on his way to the wild bramble's
shade, shifting his dustpan and broom
to one hand mid-stride and dropping
his mask to his neck before leaning into
the chest-high chain-link to reach and
eat and breathe and reach some more.
Such tenderness this afternoon: turning
to the breeze like a lover, the man closes
his eyes. So many beloveds we can't see
right now. Mine's been inside for hours,
my car the new waiting room with a view.
So many shields between us. The man's
still standing there serene as the breeze
lifts one long vine to snag his shoulder
and he turns, surprised, opens his eyes,
releases it so gently I think maybe we'll
come out of this okay. He masks his grin,
heads back into the heat that shimmers
him. The watery mirage beneath his feet
is just another thing that I can't touch.
So many of us out here mouthing our
goodbyes through glass. A father steps
between shrubs crowded around the
building, lifts his toddler to a window.
She's waving, smiling, her whole body
leaning into what she loves. What he's
helping her to reach: it's all so sweet.

I Feel You

Physics says everything is literally vibrating
an evening primrose will sense the wingbeats
of a nearby bee and boom make itself sweeter
this attraction they say is about concentration
and sugar headline news to me not those bees
on YouTube two of them in ten seconds boom
unscrewing a Fanta's cap everything is energy
that orange disc twisting the air a gasp of fizz
tingling the bottle's neck your breath on mine
before bed our evening primrose buds twitch
then shudder open wide honey everything is
blooming into bowls just waiting to be tasted
even this garden inked on me hidden flowers
you have no trouble finding in the dark

Gone Viral

First thing every day my daughter smells her toothpaste still cinnamon still healthy every day my friend's daughter asks is it over now her fourth birthday party was six chairs on their driveway two neighbors six masks and too much wind so she couldn't hear them sing and she cried because then her cake didn't taste like anything early quarantine TikTok was lousy with mothers mouthing filthy lyrics and grinning so thrilled they actually asked us of course I said yes let my daughter dress me pose me and bobblehead me I lip-synced in sunglasses pulled my pointer finger pistols from the pockets of her hand-me-downs she'll only wear mom jeans now I cuff up her old ones ready to run to her anytime guns blazing pew pew pew her clothes on me still hold her shape we do anything just to keep them close she leans over to squeal at my screen a pop-up Etsy ad custom breastmilk keepsake box yeah right sixty bucks she laughs way back to her molars her head in my lap this won't last long my Etsy cart says hurry other people want this too

America Completes Its 100-Word Interest Inventory with Permitted Items Found on TSA's "What Can I Bring?" Website

Airbrush makeup machine, antlers, artificial skeleton bones, body armor, bowling balls, breast pump, car parts, casts, cereal, Christmas lights, cigars, cologne, cooked meat, duct tape, fidget spinners, fresh eggs, glow sticks, gravy, handcuffs, Harry Potter wand, holsters, hookahs, laser hair remover, lightsaber, live lobster (transported in a clear plastic spill-proof container), lock picks, microwave, night vision goggles, parachutes (with or without Automatic Activation Devices), pet food (solid), pet food (wet), pill cutter, Play-Doh, rope, salt, selfie stick, shock collars, snow globes, tattoo guns, television, tortilla press, toys (adult), trophy, vacuum robots, waffle iron, wallet chains, wedding dress, wine bottle, Xbox.

Shout-Out to the Little Girl Bear-Walking Through TSA Security

Holiday weekend line backed way up
everyone shuffling yawning scrolling
amazing not a single person huffs not
one angles past the mother's repeated
apologies or her daughter lumbering
toward a teenager in a ripped hoodie
stamped I Woke Up Like This who's
actually crouching down now saying
hey there little bear as the girl rears up
with tiny teeth bared and giggling till
we're all waving at this surprise solo
parade that's headed for the scanner
like my friend who knows very well
those private rooms you're hurried to
when they find something suspicious
yesterday they opened her and kept
both of her breasts she texts I've tried
being fierce but who do I think I am
now the checkpoint agent is asking
the snout-to-the-ground girl's name
suddenly she jumps up fists raised
and roaring *hey it's me see I'm still me*
amazing how everyone stops texting
I'm on my way everyone's nodding
oh girl I've loved you from way back

It's Time for Them to Go Again

They move between two homes to thrive: orange gusts
of monarchs and our daughter, southbound now.
I know next spring the same ones won't come back.
Each year, she'd spot those wings ("my friends!") and run,
dropping her net—like me, it wasn't great
at letting go. I'm not sure which is worse,
this silent house or my attempts to rhyme
campus with a word that isn't virus.
They cluster by the thousands when they land.
She's easy to spot; strangers rush to touch
her hair—it's always been a glowing flare
of monarchs, settled there. Oh friends, I know.
Even across the yard, she's much too far.
She calls, and you're reminded who you are.

Mailing Care Packages on the Day the Barcelona Opera House Reopens with a Concert Exclusively for 2,292 Plants

June 2020

On red velvet they sit up straight and tender

as our children when their feet didn't reach

just yesterday they were in the nursery

the artist says voice cracking *es para ellas*

yes *this is for them* all those out there now

grown and thriving without us around

Do beavers even know what they're doing or do they just see water flowing down a river and think "absolutely not"

A beaver stands midstream in the meme
my daughter texts its little hands fisted
on its hips and muttering dam dam dam
irritated as our college town's new logo
everyone calls angry beaver its spiked
pelt and pained face ousted fan fave
retro beaver's jaunty orange cap toothy
grin speech bubble hi kids ours are so
over beaver jokes they've heard each
fall the predictable wave of students
crashing here the touchdown cannons
that's not safe my daughter liked to say
to frat boys tonguing cups sloshing by
in a DIY Chevy long-bed hot tub H-I
M-O-M shaved and pink on their pecs
absolutely not our kids eventually said
to this campus but stayed in this state
their turf-green field of first memories
if asked is your M-O-M the kind who
enjoys swimming in rivers they'd say
absolutely not they'd see me standing
there like meme beaver but shivering
maybe in their minds I've always been
cold maybe angry damn the student
newspaper tracked the last three logos
predicted an even meaner Nike beaver
next a swooshed cheek and little hand
fisted around a dagger that's not safe
I must've said sometime as angry mom
look at me when my kids look at me
how far back can they go how many
in the series of me are they able to see
popsicle mom in their hose-cold pool
endzone cheerleader mom muttering

mom hot glue fake fur beaver costume
mom do you know what you're doing
absolutely not mom red cup hot tub
Greek mom even then I was waiting
for them retro mom swimming rivers
way back a real beaver came before
the angry one and before that a man
was our mascot the kind who enjoyed
marching victorious crowds down to
the riverbank but that was ages ago so
hardly anyone here remembers that
he'd toss in his jaunty top hat carefree
as vacay mom pitching diving rings
at our kids' age I loved submerging
imagining each river's muffled rush
and sifted light as that small body
of water inside me where someday
they'd make their very first faces

Here Comes the Sun

First they floated weightless in me
Then they were out, bouncing around and planting flags

They slept above us when they slept
We'd say okay darling but it's not morning yet see

Scientists talk about light like a child, how it behaves
Out the space shuttle window the sun rises sixteen times a day

NASA broadcasts songs to say okay now you can get up
When they slept above us we'd wake to their singing

It seems like years since they've been here
We'd take turns waiting with them for light in the sky

And I'd say it's all right
Sometimes sixteen times a day

Still Life with Clear Skies and Blueberries

One place he'd sit still: under our berry-bowed branches where all he wanted fell into his lap. He's come back to us this summer. Grinning, his cheeks hold the heat-flushed toddler still alive in him. They're so good now he says.

Love Wave

> *Large earthquakes may generate Love waves that travel around the Earth several times before dissipating.*
> —Wikipedia

Goodbyes and goodnights were rough
and preschool drop-offs a total disaster
so we tried a surprise his own camera
to aim at me every time I drove away
he'd click the red button then press his
slick cheek to the window and wave
I was a mess too until his daily report
said basically mom that's not helping
he got checks by I made good choices
he made their meltdown list just once
left his camera at home and after that
each bedtime he'd cinch it to his wrist
I demonstrated problem-solving skills
said his form called hooray it's today
every night he'd ask is tomorrow the
weekend yet he'd ask for time-travel
stories just future ones he just needed
help picturing where we were going
he'd always ask mom when you end it
can you end it happy all of us okay
and can you also please make it true

Message in a Bottle: Dear Future

Stunned to still be here
after emergency brain
surgery my friend kept
weeping kept palming
her chest to feel the rise
of her actual breath oh
future maybe by now
your earth is fissured
as a cortex maybe your
West Coast has become
a sedated brain wiped
clean by waves oh dear
future if like my friend
you wake in a shaken
state may you recover
like her surrounded by
beloveds repeating the
word fine and experts
nodding at the word
stable may it be still
too soon to say what's
been irretrievably lost
may your memories
resurface like hers
just the sunny ones
floating back so far
dear future how are
you I seriously think
about you all the time

Notes

"To Tell a Different Story You Try a Different Mouth (Seismologist Cento)" is woven entirely of lines and titles exactly as they appear in the archived poetry of Charles F. Richter, creator of the earthquake magnitude scale.

The source text for "Erasing 'The Really Big One' (My Therapist Suggests I Practice Reframing)" is Kathryn Schulz's 2015 *New Yorker* article "The Really Big One," which predicts massive impending earthquakes and tsunamis for the Pacific Northwest. For this sequence I created the form of a *reverse erasure*: using the article's language exactly as printed and breaking my lines after each word or phrase I pulled from the text, I started with its very last sentence and moved towards its opening. In crafting the piece backwards, I'm invoking a more hopeful vision of the future—word by word, I reverse the article's powerful spell.

The epigraphs for "Erasing 'The Really Big One' (My Therapist Suggests I Practice Reframing)" quote Chris Goldfinger from oregonlive.com, 7/16/15, and Charles F. Richter from Susan Elizabeth Hough's biography *Richter's Scale: Measure of an Earthquake, Measure of a Man*.

About the Author

Jennifer Richter's first collection, *Threshold*, was chosen by Natasha Trethewey as a winner in the Crab Orchard Series in Poetry; Richter's second collection, *No Acute Distress*, was a Crab Orchard Editor's Selection; both were named Oregon Book Award Finalists. She was awarded a Wallace Stegner Fellowship and Jones Lectureship from Stanford University. Her recent work has been featured in ZYZZYVA, *The Los Angeles Review*, *The Missouri Review*, *The Massachusetts Review*, and other literary journals. Richter is a Chicago native who lives in Oregon's Willamette Valley and teaches in Oregon State University's MFA program. Please visit her at jenniferrichterpoet.com.

About the Artist

Vicki Jauron is an award-winning photographer specializing in moody landscapes, seascapes, birds, and wildlife. She is an advocate for conservation and has recently published her first set of children's books: *The Magical Bird Beach of Long Island* and *The Magical Bird Beach of Long Island in Winter*. Learn more at vickijauron.com.

About The Word Works

Since its founding in 1974, The Word Works has steadily published volumes of contemporary poetry and presented public programs. Its imprints include The Washington Prize, The Tenth Gate Prize, The Hilary Tham Capital Collection, and International Editions.

Monthly, The Word Works offers free programs in its Café Muse Literary Salon. Starting in 2023, the winners of the Jacklyn Potter Young Poets Competition will be presented in the June Café Muse program.

As a 501(c)3 organization, The Word Works has received awards from the National Endowment for the Arts, the National Endowment for the Humanities, the D.C. Commission on the Arts & Humanities, the Witter Bynner Foundation, Poets & Writers, The Writer's Center, Bell Atlantic, the David G. Taft Foundation, and others, including many generous private patrons.

An archive of artistic and administrative materials in the Washington Writing Archive is housed in the George Washington University Gelman Library. The Word Works is a member of the Community of Literary Magazines and Presses.

wordworksbooks.org

About the Tenth Gate Prize

The Tenth Gate Prize honors mid-career poets writing in English. Entry is open to authors of at least two previously published full-length poetry collections (excluding chapbooks, self-published volumes, and forthcoming titles). A prize of $1000 and publication of the full-length collection is awarded annually. Kasey Jueds serves as Series Editor; the winning manuscript is selected by an outside judge. The submission period is June 1 through July 15.

Leslie McGrath founded the series in 2014 to honor Jane Hirshfield's essay collection *Nine Gates: Entering the Mind of Poetry* and each winner's sustained dedication to developing a unique poetics.

Past Winners:

Jennifer Barber, *Works on Paper*, 2015
Carolyn Guinzio, *A Vertigo Book*, 2020
Christine Hamm, *Gorilla*, 2019
Lisa Lewis, *Taxonomy of the Missing*, 2017
Doug Ramspeck, *Blur*, 2021
Brad Richard, *Parasite Kingdom*, 2018
Roger Sedarat, *Haji As Puppet*, 2016
Lisa Sewell, *Impossible Object*, 2014